FIRING UP YOUR BOILER ROOM

FIRING UP YOUR BOILER ROOM

Robert Tilton

Robert Tilton Ministries
Dallas, Texas

FIRING UP YOUR BOILER ROOM
ISBN 0-914307-77-0
Copyright © 1988 by Robert Tilton Ministries
First Printing December, 1988

Published by Robert Tilton Ministries
P. O. Box 819000, Dallas, Texas 75381-9000
(Canadian Address:
P. O. Box 4900, Vancouver,
British Columbia, V6B 4A6)
Printed in the United States of America
All Rights Reserved
No Reproduction Without Permission
Editor: Kathryn P. Ingley
Cover Design: David Wilson

Contents

Studying God's Word is like shoveling coal into the boiler room of your heart, causing the fires of faith to burn higher.

Preface

God put great potential inside you, which He wants to set on fire with His Word.

You have the power to choose your destiny; it is called a will. You can have everything, be everything and do everything that you were created to have, be, and do—to be totally fulfilled in life—when you learn to listen to the still, small voice within your heart.

God has placed some good things and great desires within you. This book will show you how to release these so that you can be successful. It will open your eyes of understanding so that you can see things correctly, which is wisdom.

Everyone is looking for an honest way to provide for his or her family and to succeed in life. Since success is one of the main topics being discussed by people today, we asked several people to tell us what success meant to them.

The first person answered, "Success encompasses many things; but, basically, I want to succeed in my personal life and relationships."

The second person had a slightly different viewpoint. "I have set myself a set of goals which I am trying to reach. If I can come close to them, I will consider myself successful."

The third person answered the question this way, "My definition of success is to be happy. Most of all, I want to have a good life, a nice job, and make a decent living."

Success has many definitions ranging from feeling good to having fame and fortune, but I like to define "success" as *becoming the person you were meant to be; not trying to be someone else, but being who God created you to be*.

While everyone wants to succeed in life, not many are willing to pay the price. They want to change their circumstances, but not their lives. Many are living unfulfilled lives because they have failed to release the good things God has placed inside them. They need freedom to become who God created them to be.

Larry, the owner of some grain storage facilities, learned he had to make some changes in his life in order to become a success. By the year 1990, he and his wife could be millionaires, but it has not always been like this for Larry.

In 1982, Larry's wife began giving to the Lord through *Success-N-Life* for his salvation. She gave what she could out of the little she had, and Larry became very angry at her for doing so.

Then in 1984, Larry began having trouble with the IRS over back taxes. Their phone was disconnected, and they had very little money for food. Larry became suicidal; he thought that by killing himself, he could provide for the needs of his family.

Shortly afterward, Larry committed his life to God. At that time, he told the Lord he wanted to give to Him, but did not have any money. Twenty-four hours later, he sold a piece of equipment and gave the tithe to the Lord. He had given God his life, now he was giving Him his finances.

God has blessed him for this. Larry and his wife now give over $50,000 a year to the Lord through tithes and offerings.

The Spirit of God gave Larry an idea for leasing his grain storage facilities and making them self-supporting, instead of letting commercial elevators buy them.

Larry found that real success comes through Jesus Christ, and you will find this to be true, also. **Christ alone will bring you happiness**.

If it seems as though your life is falling apart and all hell is raging against you, you need to read this book.

Lack, confusion, and frustration are lies of the devil, and God wants to release you from them. God's Truth, as found in His Word, will set you free and allow you to see things correctly. His Word will release your faith to remove the mountains and walls of limitation which prevent His will from being done in your life.

There is a place in life where success is abundant. Just beyond sight is Heaven. God wants His will, life as it is in Heaven, to be done in your life on earth. This place is your Jericho, which means *a sweet smelling place*.

The walls surrounding Joshua's Jericho limited his entrance into the city (Joshua 6). The walls surrounding your Jericho will also keep you from getting in. This book will show you how to get rid of the walls that are stopping you from using the potential God has placed within you.

By the time you have finished reading this book, I believe you, like Joshua, will be able to shout down the walls. Then you will say with the Psalmist,

> Lift up your heads, O ye gates; and
> be ye lift up, ye everlasting doors; and
> the King of glory shall come in.
>
> Psalm 24:7

When the King of Glory comes in, salvation, healing, and prosperity also come in.

Since God has put His abilities and creativity inside you, all you need to release them is an idea from Heaven. He wants to set your spirit-man on fire with inspired ideas.

During the early years of our ministry, God gave Marte and me many inspired ideas. We were in serious financial trouble when God gave us the idea of making greeting cards.

Marte would look up the Scriptures, and I would draw the pictures. We felt sure everyone would buy four or five packs of these cards. Instead, we ended up in the red.

While driving home from a meeting in Dallas one night, I began talking to God about our problem. I said, "God, I have got to have another idea. Everybody loves these cards, but we are not selling enough of them."

If you go to God according to His Word, He will answer you.

> Call unto me, and I will answer thee, and shew thee great and mighty things, which thou knowest not.
>
> Jeremiah 33:3
>
> Ask me of things to come concerning my sons, and concerning the work of my hands command ye me.
>
> Isaiah 45:11

All of a sudden, I began to see those greeting cards in shadow boxes. Each box held seventy cards. I told Marte, "I've got it. We are not going to sell them by sevens. We are going to sell them by the rack—seventy cards in a rack."

We bought some cedar pickets and made them into 1' x 2' boxes. Marte and I gathered up cardboard from behind furniture stores and from dumpsters. Then we cut this cardboard and put it on the back of the cedar boxes. The cards and envelopes were placed inside, and we wrapped the entire rack in plastic.

On our way to a meeting, we stopped at all the book stores along the way. At every place we stopped, we sold a rack. We sold ninety per cent of those racks, making a twenty dollar profit per rack.

Sometimes we sold as many as ten racks a day. We sold those greeting cards and had enough money for gasoline, all because of an idea. Positive ideas, when captured and developed, have great energy and can bring you success.

As you read this book let it speak to your heart and ignite the fire of faith in your spirit-man.

Let's Pray

Father, You see my friends. You have made me their partner, to love them, to share my heart with them, and to teach them as You are teaching me.

Father, You see that businessman who is facing major decisions today. You see that homemaker, that couple, that woman who needs encouragement. I believe that You'll speak through me to their hearts. Show them how to release the good things You have placed within them and help them become excited about what You have for them in life. Amen.

That the communication of thy faith may become effectual by the acknowledging of every good thing which is in you in Christ Jesus.

Philemon 6

1

Understand Yourself

Through Christ you are born again of an incorruptible seed which is not subject to decay or corruption.

God's Word (His promises) are the seeds of Heaven. When they are sown in your heart, they will produce Heaven's reality in your life, which is God's will for you.

You desire beautiful things because God created you to dwell in paradise. This is why you like to:

- Smell roses and look at pretty flowers
- Have nice things around you

- Walk through well-groomed parks
- See the sparkle of the stars
- Smell good perfume
- Be surrounded by peace and harmony

God even placed a portion of Heaven on this earth in the beginning.

> That your days may be multiplied, and the days of your children, in the land which the Lord sware unto your fathers to give them, **AS THE DAYS OF HEAVEN UPON THE EARTH.**
> Deuteronomy 11:21

Then He shaped man in His image, put His Spirit in him, and placed him in the middle of that paradise called Eden.

God wanted man to enjoy his portion of Heaven on earth, so He gave him the authority to cultivate, subdue, expand, and replenish it. The spirit of life operated through him, allowing him to see things accurately, judge correctly, and deal wisely.

God did not create strife, fear, danger, anger, and jealousy. These dream stealers came into being only after Satan tempted Adam and Eve, saying,

> For God doeth know that in the day ye eat thereof [of the tree of the knowledge of good and evil], then your eyes shall be opened, and ye

> shall be as gods, knowing good and
> evil.   Genesis 3:5

Adam and Eve did not stick to the spiritual diet God designed for them. Instead, they believed Satan's lie, broke God's law, and stepped out of truth; consequently, they became carnal-minded and spiritually dead.

Since truth can only be seen through the spirit-man, Adam and Eve, who died spiritually, became blind to truth and under Satan's influence. Everything God had made for them was taken away, and the law of sin and death linked strife, fear, danger, anger and jealousy to them.

Sin ruined God's plan for their lives; and, consequently, it ruined God's plan for mankind. Adam and Eve's disobedience brought sin into the world, and it has passed down to their descendants because God had created all living things to yield seed after their own kind (Genesis 1:11, 12, 28).

A seed has three parts: (1) the embryo, (2) the food storage tissue, and (3) the seed coat. The embryo is the heart of the seed and contains its full potential for life. It is from this embryo that growth develops. A seed without an embryo, or whose embryo has died, has lost its potential for life and will not develop into a new plant.

Man is, likewise, made up of three parts—spirit, soul, and body.

> And the very God of peace sanctify
> you wholly; and I pray God your
> whole **spirit and soul and body** be
> preserved blameless unto the coming
> of our Lord Jesus Christ.
>
> I Thessalonians 5:23

These parts are not separate and discernible as the parts of a seed are, but they have separate definitions and functions.

- **Spirit** (the embryo)—the real you; the very heart of you; the spirit contains your potential for life.
- **Soul** (the food storage tissue)—the mind, the will, the power of choice, the intellect and emotions.
- **Body** (the seed coat)—the visible physical parts.

You are like a seed which has the full potential for life within itself. I have no way of knowing what type of seed you are, but I do know that within you—in your spirit—is tremendous potential. God created you in His own image (Genesis 1:26). Then when you are born again through Jesus Christ, God places within you the seed of everything He created you to be. He created your:

- potential
- creativity
- talent

God then gave you the desire to achieve your goals, fulfill your dreams, and reach your maximum potential. I am bringing these truths to you to encourage you to see yourself as you really are—as God intended you to be.

Within your physical heart is a secret place—another, a special heart, if you will—and from this heart flow the issues of your life.

> My son, attend to my words; incline thine ear unto my sayings.
>
> Let them not depart from thine eyes; keep them in the midst of thine heart.
>
> For they are life unto those that find them, and health to all their flesh.
>
> Keep thy heart with all diligence; FOR OUT OF IT ARE THE ISSUES OF LIFE.   Proverbs 4:23

This Scripture says God's Word is, literally, health and medicine to those who *find* God's Words—not to those who just *hear* them. Through His Word, you can partake of God's wisdom, strength, creativity, ability, health, peace and joy.

> According as his divine power hath given unto us all things that pertain unto LIFE and GODLINESS, through the knowledge of him that hath called us to glory and virtue:
>
> Whereby are given unto us exceeding great and **precious promises: that by these ye might be partakers**

> **of the divine nature**, having escaped
> the corruption that is in the world
> through lust.   II Peter 1:3-4

Whenever something happens which dis-
courages you, for a short while you may be
depressed. Then something begins to boil up
within your heart and continues to build up until, finally, you say, "Bless God! I'm going on.
I'm going to make it. I'm a survivor. I'm not a
partial survivor. I'm an overcomer. I will never
surrender!"

The fact that this happens shows that you
have what it takes to be the person God created
you to be. This is that spark that God has placed
within you to succeed in life. Your goal should
not be to be like me or anyone else. Your goal
should be to reach *your* maximum potential. Be
all God created you to be.

There is a warning attached to this concept,
however. Since out of your heart, your innermost
being, flow the issues of life—forces, inspiration,
creativity, and strength—it is necessary that you
guard your heart against dream stealers.

First, you must accept Jesus Christ as your
Savior. Since all seeds produce after their own
kind, all mankind since Adam have been con-
taminated by sin and controlled by Satan.

> Wherefore, as by one man sin entered
> into the world, and death by sin; and
> so death passed upon all men, for that
> all have sinned.   Romans 5:12

Before a person comes to Christ, his spirit (embryo) is dead and Satan's deceptions and illusions rule his life. Jesus said there is no truth in Satan, and He called him the father of lies (John 8:44).

A deception is a lie that misleads or directs in the wrong way. So, if truth is seeing things as they actually are, then a lie is an illusion. Therefore, anytime you step out of spiritual reality, you open yourself up to the lies of Satan.

Truth cannot be discerned by the natural mind; it can only be understood by the revelation of God which is given in His book, the Bible. For someone who was spiritually dead and who used only his carnal brain, Darwin did an outstanding job when he tried to work out the origin of creation. However, he fell far short of the truth because he relied on his natural mind, and he was wrong concerning creation.

Satan has blinded the natural mind to the truth.

> The god of this world hath blinded the minds of them which believe not, lest the light of the glorious gospel of Christ, who is the image of God, should shine unto them.
>
> II Corinthians 4:4

But Jesus, the Word, came to earth to reveal to mankind the truth about God, Heaven, and Himself, and to enable man to judge between right and wrong. He came to bring life to man's spirit and to restore his relationship with God.

I am the way, the truth, and the life.
John 14:6

For if by one man's offence death reigned by one; much more they which receive abundance of grace [restored back into a right relationship with God] and of the gift of righteousness SHALL REIGN IN LIFE BY ONE, JESUS CHRIST.
Romans 5:17

For since by man came death, by man came also the resurrection of the dead. For as in Adam all die, even so in Christ shall all be made alive.
I Corinthians 15:21-22

When you are born again, God deposits a portion of Himself in you through His incorruptible seed, Jesus. At that moment, you make Jesus Christ your Savior.

Being born again, not of corruptible seed, but of incorruptible, by the word of God, which liveth and abideth for ever.
I Peter 1:23

The Word was made flesh, and dwelt among us.
John 1:14

The day Jesus comes into your heart, you begin to live. Right then. Life does not begin when you die; it begins when you are born again. Then you begin to see things as they really are.

Through Him, you are born again of an incorruptible seed which is not subject to decay or corruption. Christ's righteousness restores you to the position God prepared for you before the fall.

Consequently, Satan's lies and deceptions can no longer influence you. No longer are you carnal-minded, but you are able to see things in relation to truth.

Jesus saves you not only from eternal death, but to a new life in Him. The word "saved" comes from the Greek word *sozo*, that means *not just forgiveness of sins, but to be an overcomer of sin and all its effects or wages.*

When you understand that the real you resides in your spirit-man, you no longer need to allow Satan to control your thoughts and desires. You can resist the powers of darkness which try to zap your creative energies, disappoint, and discourage you. You can let God's strength renew your determination to reach your goals.

When the spirit-man is responsive to God, your steps are ordered of the Lord. Therefore, with decisiveness, you can say to Satan, "I am a survivor! I am an overcomer! I am going to make it!"

The second thing you must do to guard your heart is to recognize the Lordship of Jesus in your life. This means allowing Him to lead you, step by step, into the good life He has created for you.

It means learning to listen to the voice of the Lord within you. It means hearing Him speak to you and acknowledging Him, the Greater One, inside you.

Lots of people know Jesus as Savior, and that is needful, but few allow Him to become Lord. However, you should allow Him to always be chairman of the board. He knows what is best for you, and He should be allowed to make the decisions. You should learn how to hear Him.

Proverbs 4:23 said out of your heart comes the stuff that dreams are made of. Creativity and dreams flow out of your heart. This is why it is so important to read and study God's Word. It gets down into our spirit and feeds our spirit-man. It becomes the fuel for the fires of faith.

> This book of the law shall not depart out of thy mouth; but thou shalt meditate therein day and night, that thou mayest observe to do according to all that is written therein: for then thou shalt make thy way prosperous, and then thou shalt have good success.
>
> Joshua 1:8

> So then faith cometh by hearing, and hearing by the word of God.
>
> Romans 10:17

You already have the measure of faith within you, but the promises of God ignite that faith. That seed—the potential within you—is no longer dormant.

Jesus said the kingdom of God is within you (Luke 17:21). Now we all know Heaven and hell are literal, but do we know that a portion of Heaven (God) is resident within us now? We are awakening and exciting it. When your faith is excited (or ignited), things start happening.

Have you ever gotten excited about something? That's inspiration. The Bible was written by inspiration.

> All scripture is given by inspiration of God, and is profitable for doctrine, for reproof, for correction, for instruction in righteousness.   II Timothy 3:16

God would excite a man and move through him by the inspiration of the Holy Spirit, and the man would write the Bible by truth, by revelation. God would give man the ability to see things as they actually are.

Have you ever noticed that when you really get excited about something, you start saying, "Yes, we can do this over here...and we can make that happen....We can do this..." You suddenly start seeing and understanding things. This excitement is small when compared to the feeling you experience when God excites you.

The Psalmist said, "While I was musing [meditating], the fire began to burn" (Psalm 39:3). When you meditate upon God's Words, you light fires of inspiration and faith inside yourself.

This reminds me of the boiler of the old steam engine train. When the fireman shoveled coal into the boiler, the fire burned brighter and hotter. The heat and water created the steam which moved the wheels of the train.

Studying God's Word is like shoveling coal into the boiler room of your heart where your spirit-man dwells. As you meditate on God's Word, the fire of faith burns brighter and hotter, creating actions that develop your talents and compel you forward, sweeping aside all hindering circumstances.

2

Energize Your Talents

When your talents and potential
are fired by God's Word,
things begin to happen.

As a seed has its potential stored within itself, so God has put potential within you. However, your true potential can blossom only through fellowship with Jesus Christ and His Word.

In Matthew 25, Jesus told the parable of a man traveling into a far country. Before leaving, he delivered to his servants **his goods**. To one servant he gave five talents; to another servant, two; to another, one.

God has given you **His goods**: His creativity, His power, His Name, His wisdom, His ability, His talents, and His authority to rule and reign as a king. His goods are within you now.

As you feed on God's Word, all these things within you suddenly start coming alive. No longer are they dormant; the real you becomes activated.

God's goods within you have been so suppressed, misdirected, or perverted by Satan that, in many cases, you are not even aware they are there. However, Jesus came to set you free and to bring you into the kind of life He intended for you—one of real abundance and more life than you can handle (John 10:10).

Truth brings you into this real life. Jesus is not only the Word of God (John 1:1), but He is the Truth, the Way and the Life (John 14:6). It is His responsibility, therefore, to produce in you real life.

In order to do this, He has first given you the written Word, to profit you both in the present and in the future.

> All scripture is given by inspiration of God, and is profitable for doctrine, for reproof, for correction, for instruction in righteousness.   II Timothy 3:16

If you have wandered off course, the Word of God will bring you back and instruct you in righteousness. "Righteousness" means *walking in agreement with God's truth; meeting the*

*standards of what is morally right and just; be-
ing right with God.*

> My son, attend to my words; incline
> thine ear unto my sayings.
>
> Let them not depart from thine
> eyes; keep them in the midst of thine
> heart.
>
> For they are life unto those that
> find them, and health to all their flesh.
>
> Proverbs 4:20-22

> Meditate upon these things; give thy-
> self wholly to them; that thy profiting
> may appear to all.
>
> I Timothy 4:15

Truth is *the quality of being in agreement
with reality or fact*. When you meditate upon
God's Word, it brings you into agreement with
reality and multiplies your potential a hundred
times over (Mark 10:29-30).

The servants who were given five and two
talents, doubled the values of their talents. Likewise, as you develop the potential God has given
you, it will grow and multiply.

The servant who was given one talent kept
it buried in the earth (in himself), because of fear
(verse 25). Some people are afraid of failing, and
so they do nothing. Instead of success, they end
up with nothing but their fear.

God wants you to uncover your buried
potential, so that it can grow and multiply within
you.

According as his divine power hath given unto us all things that pertain unto life and godliness, through the knowledge of him that hath called us to glory and virtue:

Whereby are given unto us exceeding great and precious promises: that by these ye might be partakers of the divine nature, having escaped the corruption that is in the world through lust.   II Peter 1:3-4

God told Joshua, before he entered into the Promised Land, that he should meditate upon the book of the law [Word of God] day and night "that thou mayest **observe to do according to all that is written therein**: for **then** thou shalt make thy way prosperous, and **then** thou shalt have good success" (Joshua 1:8).

Meditating (thinking and dwelling in thought) on the Scriptures will fuel and light a fire within you. When God's Word is absorbed into your spirit-man, it will bring your talents and abilities to life. Then you will become a partaker of God's:

- Wisdom
- Strength
- Power
- Authority
- Creativity
- Ability

- Health
- Peace
- Joy
- Inspiration

God blesses those who diligently seek Him, and His Word changes their lives for the better. Meditating on the Word of God renews the mind to the will of God as it is in Heaven and de-emphasizes natural circumstances.

Jesus Christ came to show you life as it is in Heaven. That is why He prayed, ''Thy will be done in earth, as it is in heaven'' (Matthew 6:10). Because of this, you could say, ''The will of God, as it is in Heaven, came to the earth.'' Every time He healed someone, Jesus released God's will into his or her life.

There is no lack or shortage in Heaven, and Jesus proved this by feeding the multitude. When He multiplied the five loaves and two fishes (Matthew 14:15-21), He released the will of God into the lives of those people.

There is no sickness or disease in Heaven; therefore, when Jesus delivered the people from devils, lunacy, convulsions, epilepsy, and palsy, He was releasing health as it is in Heaven into their lives.

If you will believe and claim them, there are about 7,000 promises in the Bible—one for every situation you face—that will release the will of God into your life.

Like the man in the parable, God has placed His goods—His talents—within you. You have the opportunity of seeing what you can do with them. You have the choice of burying them within your fears or energizing them by the inspiration of God's Word.

3

Use Your Power of Choice

Incorrect information from your senses can cause you to make wrong choices.

When I first received Christ as my Savior, I read a lot about Heaven and the rapture. The general feeling, in those days, was, "One of these days it is going to be better, for the rapture will come."

I remember praying for several consecutive nights that the rapture would come that night; I wanted so much to go to Heaven. Later, I found out that Heaven wanted to come to me.

God has given us the keys to release the will of God into the earth and our lives.

> And I will give you the keys of the kingdom of heaven: and whatsoever thou shalt bind on earth shall be bound in heaven: and whatsoever thou shalt loose on earth shall be loosed in heaven.   Matthew 16:19

Jesus said, "the kingdom of God is within you" (Luke 17:21). I know there is a literal Heaven and hell, but there is also a portion of Heaven within you.

Man was created to live in paradise, but Satan deceived him, causing him to lose everything God created for him. Satan came into the world illegally, and he has tried to blind people to the truth ever since. He is still trying to deceive and destroy you with his illusions.

The Prophet Jonah says, "They that observe lying vanities [life's illusions] forsake their own mercy" (Jonah 2:8). The Emphasized Bible, a translation by J.B. Rotherham, states it this way, "They who take heed to the vanities of falsehood do their own lovingkindness forsake." Think about it! Those who listen to Satan's false information or look at surrounding circumstances are forsaking their own mercy and destroying their strength.

> When a strong man armed keepeth his palace, his goods are in peace.

> But when a stronger than he shall
> come upon him, and overcome him,
> he taketh from him all his armour
> wherein he trusted, and divideth his
> spoils [goods].   Luke 11:21-22

There are two ways of looking at things: (1) the carnal way, which is by using the five senses, or (2) the spiritual way, which is by using God's Word. This does not mean you need to stop using your five senses. It means the information gained from the senses needs to be balanced with spiritual insight and values.

The unbalanced carnal senses allow Satan's lies and illusions to mislead you. For example, some people think sickness and lack are normal. This is both an illusion and a lie. It is Satan's way of preventing man from possessing the blessings of God.

Satan, the god of this world, is a thief, and he is trying to steal your heavenly life. He does not want you to know what truth and reality are. He does not want you to know that Jesus came so that you can have life more abundantly.

> I am the door: by me if any man enter
> in, he shall be saved, and shall go in
> and out, and find pasture.
>
> The thief cometh not, but for to
> steal, and to kill, and to destroy: I am
> come that they might have life, and
> that they might have it more abun-
> dantly.   John 10:9-10

> The god of this world hath blinded the minds of them which believe not, lest the light of the glorious gospel of Christ, who is the image of God, should shine unto them.
>
>   II Corinthians 4:4

During Christ's crucifixion there was an earthquake, and the veil of the temple was rent (Matthew 27:51). This splitting of the veil signified that no longer is man justified and made righteous by the sacrificing of a lamb, but man's righteousness is only in Jesus Christ, the lamb of God without spot or blemish (I Peter 1:19).

Through Christ, all that Satan stole from man has been restored. Man justified through Christ can now claim his inheritance. With Christ's resurrection, Satan was totally defeated. The seed of woman had bruised the head of the serpent (Genesis 3:15).

Mark 5:25-34 tells of a woman who had an issue of blood for 12 years. When she touched Jesus, the will of God and truth released her. Jesus said, ''Ye shall know the truth, and the truth shall make you free'' (John 8:32).

Free from what? Free from the lies of Satan. When Adam stepped out of truth, Satan and his lies took dominion over all mankind. Now, God's grace and His gift of righteousness give you the victory over Satan. Truth has authority over the devil. Jesus is the truth (John 14:6).

Because the Word of God is truth, it releases you from lies and deceptions. It gives you choices. It teaches you to judge between right and wrong, truth and lies, light and darkness, and good and evil.

When you meditate on God's Word, you are taking in heavenly information and truth, whereby you gain wisdom. Then when sickness or lack come, you can say, "My mind is no longer blinded, and my eyes are no longer closed. I know God gives me health and abundance."

The Word of God gives you choices regarding your behavior. People generally react to situations according to their emotions, feelings, or senses. They seem unaware that many times your senses will lie to you and prevent you from hearing the voice of God. It is necessary, therefore, that you diligently guard your heart against making choices based on the way circumstances may appear from natural observation.

> For as he [a man] thinketh in his heart,
> so is he.   Proverbs 23:7

The choices you make determine the quality of your life. Since you have the power of choice, you can accept things as they are or you can look for a better solution.

Christopher Columbus found his place in life because he listened to his heart before making his choice. His dream came from his heart and was ignited as he read God's Word. He found Scripture that talked about the world being round, not square as the scientists of his day believed. He found Scriptures that talked about horizons and many different things. The Bible illuminated his understanding, and his faith allowed him to see the impossible.

> Faith cometh by hearing, and hearing
> by the word of God.
>
> Romans 10:17

His faith showed him some things in the Word of God, and he could not sleep or rest until he established that the world was round. He wanted to find a new world; he wanted to find a shorter sea route to the Indies and establish a new city for trading.

As much as he tried to shake that desire, he just couldn't do it. God put that desire in his heart and it lighted his being. According to Job, your spirit is like a lamp which God has lighted to give you the ability to see what you have within you.

> There is a spirit in man: and the in-
> spiration of the Almighty giveth them
> understanding.   Job 32:8

Upon his return to his home after discovering the new world, Columbus was given a party by his peers and friends. Many of them were jealous of his great exploits, and said, "Oh, we could have done that."

Columbus picked up an egg and asked, "Which one of you can balance this egg on its end?" The egg was passed around the table, but no one could balance it.

When they had all failed, Columbus took a spoon, tapped one end of the egg, and stood it on end.

"Oh, that's nothing," they remarked. "We could have done that too, if we had thought of it."

"Yes, that is the difference between you and me," Columbus answered. "I thought of it and did it. You did not think of it; or even if you did think of it, you did not do it."

Like Columbus, you have dreams and ideas inside you that need to be released.

> For where your treasure is, there will
> your heart be also.   Matthew 6:21

The other day I was meditating on this Scripture when suddenly the words switched places. Then the Scripture read this way, "Where your heart is, there is where your treasure is also." The words of this Scripture are interchangeable, because your heart is where your treasure is, and your treasure is where your heart is. All treasure starts first in Heaven (the spiritual) then flows to the natural.

Where is your heart? Remember, out of your heart flow the issues of life (Heaven's will). Those dreams and ideas which lie buried deep within you are your treasures.

Some people will go to any lengths to search for buried treasure. Years ago, a minister named Russell Conwell preached what many consider one of the world's greatest sermons. It has been said that this sermon has been preached more times than any other. It has been duplicated on tapes, written in books, and read by people all over the world. It was so good that even those who didn't believe in God discovered and used it for the wisdom it contained. The title of the sermon is ''Acres of Diamonds,'' and the message is this:

A man had a farm, but it wasn't enough. He wanted to be rich with diamonds. He wanted to find great wealth, so he sold his farm to travel around the world in his quest for the great treasure he desired; but he later died a pauper.

In the meantime, the man who bought the farm was out by the creek one day. He happened to look down just as the sun caught something sparkling on the ground. He picked it up to discover that it was a beautiful diamond.

That one diamond turned out to be one of the most valuable diamonds ever discovered, and the farm became the world's most famous diamond mine.

The original owner was traveling all over the world searching for riches, but they were in his own backyard all the time—he just didn't know it.

People travel all over the world to find their place and purpose in life and to capture success, but all along it is inside them, like a seed waiting to be cultivated.

Where your heart is, that is where your treasure will be found. What are you interested in?

> Delight thyself also in the Lord; and he shall give thee the desires of thine heart.
>
> Commit thy way unto the Lord; trust also in him; and he shall bring it to pass.   Psalm 37:4-5

God has placed His treasure in you; His wisdom and creative abilities are in you. Christ, the Son of God, is resident within you. As you delight yourself in Him, you will begin to discover these treasures within.

What are the desires of your heart? Desires are things you have been longing to do. I am not talking about fleshly desires; I am talking only about things that line up with the will of God.

You can have the desires of your heart, when your mind is renewed by the Word of God. When you put God first and delight yourself in Him, He will release those desires and inspirations. He'll cause you to become so excited about them that they will bubble up inside you.

Jesus taught us to pray, ''Give us this day our daily bread'' (Matthew 6:11). God knows you need money for food. Where does money come from? From work. Where does work come from? From meeting a need. But it *all* comes from an idea. Therefore, we can pray, ''Give us this day our daily inspiration.'' Since all Scripture is given by inspiration of God, when we feed on the Word we become partakers of divine inspiration.

When you believe God's Word, then God becomes a BIG God. No longer is He a God of the past or future, but He is God of the NOW.

The devil has tried to keep people ignorant of the things God has placed within them. He also has tried to make God small, so that people will not believe He can do anything. But Satan is a liar. God is so BIG, NOTHING is impossible for Him (Mark 10:27)!

4

Monitor Your Gatekeeper

*Your will is the gatekeeper that controls
every area of your life, health, marriage,
and finances.*

Many people react to situations according
to their emotions or senses, failing to
realize that senses may lie. Lying
senses will prevent you from hearing God. God's
Word, however, will help you make decisions
without relying on your senses.

> For as he [a man] thinketh in his heart
> [soul], so is he.
>
> Proverbs 23:7

The word "think" means *to reason, to judge, to draw deductions*. "To judge" means *to choose wisely*.

When your senses give you incorrect information, you will make wrong decisions. Every area of your life is limited by your reason and judgment.

The Hebrew word for heart is *nephesh,* which means *soul* and includes the will, the mind, the intellect, the emotions and the power of choice. The gatekeeper of your soul is your will which controls every area of your life, health, marriage, and finances.

Information gathered through your senses is judged by your will before it determines what portions of the information are allowed to remain.

> That the communication of thy faith may become effectual by the acknowledging of every good thing which is in you in Christ Jesus.
>
> Philemon 1:6

Those inspired ideas inside you cannot produce until you allow them to exit into life. Therefore, when you say "yes" to them, you open the gate and allow them to flow out. As you start releasing the good things God has given you, He will give you more.

Your will can become distorted and limit the exit of these ideas, however, when you go by natural circumstances. For this reason, it is important that you post the Word of God on the door of your will to guard it against the desires of the flesh.

> And thou shalt write them upon the door posts of thine house, and upon thy gates.

> That your days may be multiplied, and the days of your children, in the land which the Lord sware unto your fathers to give them, as the days of heaven upon the earth.
>
> > Deuteronomy 11:20-21

> I beseech you therefore, brethren, by the mercies of God, that ye present your bodies a living sacrifice, holy, acceptable unto God, which is your reasonable service.

> And be not conformed to this world: but be ye transformed by the renewing of your mind, that ye may prove what is that good, and acceptable, and perfect, will of God.
>
> > Romans 12:1-2

When the Word is posted at the entrance of your will, it renews your mind; it keeps the bad out and lets the good in; it lengthens your life; it governs the carnal mind; it controls ideas and motivations.

Your biggest battles are in your mind because the forces of evil attack your thinking. Romans

8:7 says the carnal mind wars against the spiritual mind. However, since your will is the gatekeeper of your mind, you can control what enters and leaves it.

The kingdom of God is within you. The potential is there for everything God created you to be. Your potential is just waiting for you to release it.

Harold retired from his job early so he could release his potential. He and his wife took their life savings and bought a broken down laundromat.

They worked twenty-four hours a day fixing it up. When they had that one operating smoothly, they bought another laundromat. When each laundromat became functional, they would buy another, and another, and another.

By reading God's Word, Harold learned who he was in Christ; therefore, he could deal wisely in the affairs of his life. When your life is based on God's Word, it is easy to keep things running smoothly.

When God's truth daily renews your mind, you can then listen to the good things and reject the bad. Truth allows you to shut the door to the lies of the devil, but open it to the things of God. The decision is yours, but to be a quality gatekeeper you need wisdom.

Wisdom allows you to see things in relation to truth, to deal wisely and to judge between truth and error, and good and evil. ''Wisdom'' means *the ability to see things as they actually are; to see things correctly*.

Some Christians still give heed to what is going on around them. They have not yet learned to listen to the voice of the Lord saying, "This is the way. This is what I have called you to do. I have this inspired idea for you."

Revelation 3:20 says, "Behold, I stand at the door, and knock." What is the door? It is your will. Only you can make the decision to let Christ in or keep Him out. The Psalmist put into words what happens when Jesus stands at the door (drawbridge) of your heart and says:

> Lift up your heads, O ye gates; and be ye lift up, ye everlasting doors; and the King of glory shall come in.
>
> Who is this King of glory? The LORD strong and mighty, the LORD mighty in battle.
>
> Lift up your heads, O ye gates; even lift them up, ye everlasting doors; and the King of glory shall come in.
>
> Who is this King of glory? The LORD of hosts, he is the King of glory.
>
> Psalms 24:7-10

Your body is the temple of God (II Corinthians 6:16). When the enemy knocks at your door, you do not have to let him in. As gatekeeper, you can let in what you want and keep out what you want kept out.

5

Regulate Your
Mind and Senses

A mind left to itself is powerless; but when your thinking is brought under control, there is great power.

Several years ago, there were six teenage suicides in a little town of 22,000 people, located just outside of Houston. Why did these youth kill themselves? Because the lies and deceptions of Satan had taken over their wills through their minds, causing them to take their lives.

Recently, television carried a movie, called ''The Burning Bed,'' about a man who beat his wife. Afterwards, hideous things happened across America because of what people saw in that movie. One man poured gasoline over his wife while she slept and set her on fire.

Why? What causes suicide and wife abuse? People have carnal minds and do not know how to control their thinking (Romans 8:7). No one has told them about the enemy who is bombarding their minds with negative thoughts.

Remember how seriously you took things when you were a teenager? I remember I felt like the end of the world had come when I got into trouble. Teenagers today are forced to face much more severe problems—problems more suitable to adults than to teens. They also face stronger peer pressure than we did.

A common weakness in mankind is the inability to control their thinking. Many people let all kinds of thoughts—most of them negative—pass through their minds. Eventually, those thoughts rule their lives.

Some Christians are not even sure whether they should use their minds. They fear that using their minds might hinder their spirituality. However, they forget God created their minds and gave them memory, will power, and the power of choice.

A mind left to itself is powerless because it continually wanders; but when you harness your thinking and bring it under control, there is great power.

> Finally, brethren, whatsoever things
> are true, whatsoever things are honest,
> whatsoever things are just, whatsoever
> things are pure, whatsoever things are
> lovely, whatsoever things are of good
> report; if there be any virtue, and if
> there be any praise, think on these
> things.   Philippians 4:8

Einstein, the scientific genius, used only 10 per cent of his mental capacity, according to studies that were done on his brain. The average person uses between 6 to 8 per cent of his mental capacity. It required a little extra thinking for Einstein to originate his many theories and inventions.

It has been proven that within twenty-four hours you forget approximately 25 per cent of what you heard that day. Within forty-eight hours, 50 per cent. Within four days, roughly 80 per cent. By the end of sixteen days, you have forgotten 98 per cent of what you heard.

This is true because your mind wanders when you begin listening to someone or something. It begins by going over things that happened during the day, or things that you are going to do. All kinds of thoughts distract your mind from its course.

> An idle soul shall suffer hunger
>   Proverbs 19:15

The word "idle" means *moving aimlessly*. In other words, an idle mind is alive, but it is not going in any particular direction. It is moving aimlessly with no destination or plan. "Idle" also means *operating without transmitting power*. The mind is there, but it is not really doing anything. Apathy has set in, leaving it without purpose or direction.

Approximately 95 per cent of the people of the world move aimlessly through life, without purpose or direction. Otherwise, they would be doing more powerful and exciting things with their lives.

An idle soul has no hope and suffers hunger. The word "hunger" means *weakness caused by lack of food*. Allowed to be alone and not directed, your mind will hunger for information. A soul left to itself, will suffer hunger and weakness from a lack of creative ideas or inspirational thoughts.

God wants each individual to reach his maximum potential. Your purpose in life is *not* to be like anyone else, but to be everything God created you to be. God did not create you to float aimlessly, like a feather on the air currents. Instead, He created you to use your will power, to compel the fulfillment of your dreams.

The Bible has quite a lot to say about thinking.

> When I was a child, I spake as a child,
> I understood as a child, I thought as

a child: but when I became a man, I
put away childish things.

I Corinthians 13:11

Remember, when you first got saved how,
because of immaturity, you would let anything
come out of your mouth? You spoke like a child.
"Woe is me. What are we going to do now? I
feel terrible. We don't have any money. Nobody
likes me."

Perhaps, you still have some signs of immaturity because you have not learned to bridle
your tongue (James 3:2-10). Therefore, you are
having severe problems:

- Financial
- Marital
- Spiritual
- Physical

This is because the only information you are
receiving comes through your carnal senses, and
that is limited.

Many Christians are living depressed lives
because they are beaten down by the devil. Their
minds are not harnessed or controlled.

Carnal-minded Christians are also double
minded, floating whichever way the wind blows.
One minute they listen to the will of God, and
the next minute they listen to their carnal senses.

Carnal-minded Christians have not learned
to build their lives upon the solid foundation of
God's Word. Consequently, their lives—marriage, finances, health and conversation—are

unstable. The Scripture says we should see with eyes of wisdom, not natural eyes, so that we may build solid lives. "The wise man's eyes are in his head" (Ecclesiastes 2:14).

> That the God of our Lord Jesus Christ, the Father of glory, may give unto you the spirit of wisdom and revelation in the knowledge of him:
>
> The eyes of your understanding being enlightened [opened]; that ye may know what is the hope of his calling [the purpose of Jesus' coming], and what the riches of the glory of his inheritance in the saints.
>
> Ephesians 1:17-18

God wants your eyes open so you will understand the importance of Jesus' death and resurrection. He wants you to understand what it meant to your spirit-man when the veil in the temple was torn from top to bottom (Matthew 27:51).

Most Christians only hope to be like Jesus. But when you read God's Word and find out He is already inside you and has given you an inheritance, your faith grows.

When your spirit-man hears the Word of God, he wakes up. Suddenly, you are not beaten down any longer for faith is rising up in your heart. The Word is God's manual for success and will give you instructions in right:

- Believing
- Thinking
- Talking
- Living

As you accept the Word of God by faith, it purifies your spirit from sin and brings health to your body. It is God's will that you be sanctified and preserved blameless until the second coming of Jesus.

> And the very God of peace sanctify you wholly; and I pray God your whole spirit and soul and body be preserved blameless unto the coming of our Lord Jesus Christ.
>
> I Thessalonians 5:23

The word "sanctify" means to *purify; to make free from sin; to make free from error*.

Some people teach that God sanctifies you by sending you problems. Are you guilty of saying, "Well, I guess God is trying to teach me something?" God is not trying to teach you something, but the devil is trying to steal what you have.

Perhaps you have even asked, "Well, doesn't God purge us so we can bring forth more fruit?"

> Every branch in me that beareth not fruit he taketh away: and every branch that beareth fruit, he purgeth it, that it may bring forth more fruit.

> Now ye are clean through the
> word which I have spoken unto you.
> John 15:2-3

You are purged (sanctified) by the washing of the Word of God (Ephesians 5:26), which causes you to bring forth more fruit.

> I beseech you therefore, brethren, by the mercies of God, that ye present your bodies a living sacrifice, holy, acceptable unto God, which is your reasonable service.
>
> And be not conformed to this world: but be ye transformed by the renewing of your mind, that ye may prove what is that good, and acceptable, and perfect, will of God.
> Romans 12:1-2

Paul urges you to present your emotions and senses to God as a living sacrifice. When you offer God all your senses, His Word eliminates your *negative* emotions. Then your mind is renewed and your thinking is transformed. No longer will you be conformed to the world's system. No longer are you influenced by this world's negative feedback. Your spirit-man is alive because Christ lives in you. Therefore, you can now think like God wants you to think.

You present your senses to God so that you will not be conformed to lack, poverty, sickness, disease, fear, discouragement, turmoil, anxieties, guilt, and limitation. God never created this earth for lack; He created the earth for abundance. Many people, however, refuse to believe the abundance is theirs and they do without all their lives.

A group of researchers, who were studying the conditioning process, placed many minnows and a large pike in one aquarium. Pike is a fresh-water game fish which thrives on minnows. Naturally, the pike feasted on those little minnows.

Then, the scientists put a pane of glass across the middle of the aquarium so the new minnows they added were on one side of the glass, and the pike was on the other. The partition remained in place for several weeks. The pike tried to get the minnows, but he just hit his head on the glass. He saw the minnows, but he couldn't get to them.

Then one day the scientists pulled out the glass. The pike swam freely all around the minnows, but he didn't eat even one of them. He had been conditioned by the presence of the glass, so he just assumed he couldn't eat minnows anymore.

Eventually, the pike died of starvation. He was surrounded by abundance, but he believed he could no longer eat. If the pike had stopped going by how things looked, he could have eaten a batch of minnows and lived. Instead, he died of starvation in the midst of plenty.

In the same way, you become conditioned:
- to lack
- to insurmountable problems
- to sickness
- to failure

Satan wants you to believe that you will always be poor and sick. He wants you to think that you are a failure. The truth is: You are someone special, and you have great potential within you.

You are not limited by high prices and inflation. All you need are good ideas from Heaven. God has already placed within you His abilities and His creativity, and, as your thinking is changed by the Word of God, you will hear the voice of the godly desires of your heart.

Some people call this voice a hunch, an inner feeling or intuition; whatever you may call it, it is God's voice teaching you from within so that He can give you the desires of your heart. The secret is learning to hear.

Romans 12:2 says ''ye may **prove** what is that good, and acceptable, and perfect, will of God.'' ''Prove'' means *to establish as truth; to establish the validity of; to produce desired results; to enforce*. Basically, you renew your mind to truth so that you can think correctly and establish God's will in the earth. You renew your mind to truth, joy, creativity, peace, gentleness, meekness, and longsuffering. You are literally learning to walk in the Spirit of God, for the kingdom of God is not meat and drink, but righteousness, peace and joy in the Holy Spirit.

You renew your mind to truth so that you won't be like that pike fish who wouldn't eat the minnows. There are minnows all around you—love, abundance, health, inspired ideas—ready for the taking.

Respond to the desires in your heart. Listen to the voice in your heart and find your treasure. Now, please notice, I am not teaching you to respond to lustful desires or carnal knowledge. I am teaching you to respond to revelation knowledge that God gives you, along with godly desires. If your desires, in any way, conflict with the Word of God, then you need to back up and re-examine your motivation and desires.

When your mind is renewed by the Word of God, your motivation and desires will be pure. Then this world's beggarly elements cannot limit you, and God will release His will, abundance and blessings into your life. The prodigal son's brother was angry because the prodigal enjoyed his father's blessings and abundance when he returned home (Luke 15:11-32). The world does not want God to bless you, but God wants to bless you, even as He blessed Abraham.

> That in blessing I will bless thee, and
> in multiplying I will multiply thy seed
> as the stars of the heaven.
> Genesis 22:17

God's desire is that His will be done on earth as it is in Heaven. He also wants to renew your mind to:

- Joy
- Creativity
- Peace
- Gentleness
- Longsuffering
- Meekness

When your mind is renewed, you will think correctly and God's will can be manifested in your life. Then you can release His will into the earth. Jesus operated in God's will and manifested God in the earth.

> Jesus answered: "Don't you know me, Philip, even after I have been among you such a long time? ANYONE WHO HAS SEEN ME HAS SEEN THE FATHER. How can you say, 'Show us the Father'?"
>
> John 14:9 (NIV)

When our carnal senses are placed on the altar, Heaven opens to you. If you want everything God has for you, then "be not conformed to this world" (Romans 12:2).

> The carnal mind is enmity against God: for it is not subject to the law of God, neither indeed can be.
>
> Romans 8:7

"Enmity" is *a deep-seated hatred, hostility or antagonism*. The carnal mind is hostile toward the Spirit of God. Therefore, the carnal senses are against everything Jesus came to give you because the flesh is sinful. Many people make decisions for Christ, but fail to put their senses on the altar. They still want their senses appeased, and refuse to change their thinking.

This world's lying vanities will not bother you, when your senses are on the altar. Also, when your thinking is transformed, Satan's "fiery darts" will not hurt you.

The pike fish died because he refused to change his thinking! By changing your thinking you can prove what is the perfect will of God for you (Romans 12:2).

God wants you to prove Him and release Him, so humanity can see who He is through you. God has given you the responsibility of manifesting His will as it is in Heaven. He said that if you will prove Him, He would "open the windows of Heaven" to you (Malachi 3:10).

By using the keys of the kingdom, you can release Heaven into the earth, thus showing mankind what earth was like when God originally created it for man.

I Samuel 17 tells how Goliath defied the armies of Israel. Yelling at them, he filled them with lies until the whole camp cowed in fear.

David refused to listen to Goliath's lies. Instead he listened to the truth of God. When

David defeated Goliath, truth prevailed and the armies of Israel were set free.

Truth still prevails over sickness, disease, discouragement, and all negative thoughts. Truth knows that only through Christ in you will you reach your maximum potential in life.

> Now unto him that is able to do exceeding abundantly above all that we ask or think, according to the power that worketh in us.
>
> Ephesians 3:20

God has given you the responsibility of bringing to others:
- Plenty out of lack
- Joy out of sorrow
- Health out of sickness
- Life out of death.

> Finally, brethren, whatsoever things are true, whatsoever things are honest, whatsoever things are just, whatsoever things are pure, whatsoever things are lovely, whatsoever things are of good report; if there be any virtue, and if there be .any praise, think on these things.
>
> Those things, which ye have both learned, and received, and heard, and seen in me, do: AND THE GOD OF PEACE SHALL BE WITH YOU.
>
> Philippians 4:8-9

Let's Pray

Oh, God in Heaven, forgive us of our mistakes, the times we have stepped out of truth and into the deceptions and lies of Satan. We repent so the thief, the father of lies, will no longer steal from us.

Jesus, wash us clean now. We put You on the throne of our hearts. We confess You as our Lord, provider, caretaker, and director. Thank You, Father. In Jesus' Name. Amen

6

Release Your Positive Ideas

*An inspired idea carries with it an element
of faith which starts a chain reaction
of belief, making its fulfillment possible.*

Thousands of inspired ideas surround you every day. When, through the Word of God, you partake of God's inspiration, your spirit is lighted, causing you to see, hear, and understand those inspired ideas.

> The spirit of man is the candle of the
> Lord, searching all the inward parts of
> the belly.   Proverbs 20:27

An ''idea'' is *something that exists in the
mind, the product of mental activity, a thought*

or a mental image, the ability to see something.

Recently, I read an article which stated that the average individual has over two thousand ideas a day pass though his mind. Sadly, most of these ideas receive no attention because we have not trained ourselves to know which ones need to be developed or which should be shelved.

Not all ideas are positive; some are destructive. Therefore, it is important to know the difference between them and to immediately discard all destructive ideas.

After reading this article, I added up the number of new ideas I had in one month. My range was from fifteen to twenty strong ideas. These ideas only came when I was in a receptive and sensitive attitude.

Many years ago, a mechanic who earned twenty dollars a week received an inspired idea. This idea, the mass production of the automobile, revolutionized the entire automobile industry. In twenty years that man became the wealthiest man in all the world. His name was Henry Ford.

In another state, a man was sitting on his front porch, watching his cat trying to get into his canary's cage. Suddenly, the idea of how to separate cotton from its seed came to him. This man was Eli Whitney, and he invented the cotton gin.

Another young man who was talented in the area of color combinations wanted to do something to help humanity. He concluded he could best do this by using his colors on women's faces. He took this idea, and by releasing his talent, developed it. His idea became a multimillion dollar business. This man was Charles Revson, the founder of the Revlon Corporation.

Several years ago while I was reading Isaiah 55, I had a vision of a satellite raining God's Word down from Heaven. Like sheets of rain, God's Word swept across the North American continent and around the world.

This revelation was the beginning of our Satellite seminars and our *Success-N-Life* programs. Today, our *Success-N-Life* programs are broadcast across North America.

A few years ago God showed me from Proverbs 16:3, how to receive inspired ideas.

> Roll your works upon the Lord—
> commit and trust them wholly to Him;
> [He will cause your thoughts to
> become agreeable to His will, and] so
> shall your plans be established and
> succeed.   Proverbs 16:3 (AMP)

When God first gave me that Scripture, I meditated on it night and day until I had totally given my works to God.

Marte and I had only been in the ministry a short time, and we were not doing well financially. We were living on beans and corn bread

and had no money for gasoline. To the carnal
senses it looked like we had reached the end of
our ministry.

Marte was wondering if we should have ever
gone into the ministry. She said, "Something is
wrong, Bob; you are not working." Then she
read this Scripture to me,

> But if any provide not for his own, and
> specially for those of his own house,
> he hath denied the faith, and is worse
> than an infidel.   I Timothy 5:8

She had found it in the Bible, so there was
not much I could say. My job was to preach. If
I was not preaching, then I was not working.
This was quite serious to me because I had been
studying Proverbs 16:3.

When I went to bed that night I said, "Lord,
I have given my works to You; now You have got
to move. We have got to have a solution."
Deuteronomy 4:29 in the Amplified Version says,
"You will find Him, if you [truly] seek Him with
all your heart [and mind] and soul and life."

When I woke up the next morning the Lord
said to me, "Paul had a tent making job." I did
not want to hear those words. Suddenly, the idea
of putting up cedar fences entered my mind.

Marte and I bought an old pick-up truck. It
was really ugly, but it beat walking. Then I
applied at a fence company. The owner asked
if I had ever built a fence before? I said, "No,
but I have watched others. If they can do it, I
can do it."

I must have convinced him because he gave me a load of fence pickets. Then he said, "Go build a fence. Here is the address, but I want to see what it looks like when you are finished."

Marte and I put the pickets in the truck; then we bought a few other pieces of equipment that we needed. I had never used a power saw in my life, but we had confidence in God.

We got the fence up, but had trouble putting the gate on. Finally, we finished the fence and had to rebuild only a small section. The owner must have felt we did a good job, because he gave us another fence to build.

God blessed us in that work and showed us how to "roll our works upon the Lord." He also taught us to let our thoughts be in agreement with His will.

Ideas may come as a hunch which is *a strong thought, or intuitive feeling*. "Intuition" is *the act of knowing without the use of rational process, or to be taught from within*. This is a form of inspiration.

> But there is a spirit in man: and the inspiration of the Almighty giveth them understanding [will tell you what to do]. Job 32:8

According to II Timothy 3:16, the whole Bible was given by the inspiration of God. While God did not call you to write the Bible, the same anointing the prophets had can be yours. One tiny idea, given by God, can become something potentially great.

Not long ago a Presbyterian minister had a big idea that he could not shake. His idea was to build a trade school for those who could not afford to go to a regular school.

He became consumed by this idea, but it would cost a million dollars to build the school. He did not have a million dollars. All he had were about a hundred people in his church, and none of them was wealthy.

The devil tormented him with the fact that he did not have a million dollars. Then another idea came to him. He ran a full page announcement of his Sunday morning message: "What I Would Do If I Had a Million Dollars."

When he came to church Sunday morning, the building was filled. Everyone wanted to find out what he would do if he had a million dollars.

At the end of the service an elderly man came to him and said, "Sir, Monday morning I will have a check for you for one million dollars." That man was Frank Armour, the owner of the Armour Meat Packing Company. That school is known today as Illinois Institute of Technology (IIT) and has thousands of students enrolled. This all happened because one man dared to have an idea and a BIG dream. All ideas have enough potential within them to bring success.

What would you do if you had a million dollars? What would you do if you knew whatever you dreamed would come to pass? What would you dream?

Ideas many times come as words of wisdom. "Wise" means *the ability to see*. Real wisdom is having your mind opened to the fact that it is, "Christ in you, the hope of glory" (Colossians 1:27), as well as the fact that God created all things for Himself, then gave them to us (Revelation 4:11).

God wants you to understand that when Christ is in you, then the mind of Christ is in you (Philippians 2:5). Therefore, you can draw ideas out of the mind of Christ.

I receive ideas all the time. Some I keep, and some I give away because I have more than I can handle. Ideas are constantly coming into my mind because the mind of Christ is operating in my life.

God wants to give you an idea, but you must not limit your thinking. Psalms 78:41 states that the children of Israel limited God. Ideas must be received by faith. If your faith is small, you may fail to receive them. If you think small, do not expect God to give you big ideas. When you learn to think big, then God will give you big ideas.

The kingdom of God inside you *will* bring forth fruit (ideas) of itself (Mark 4:28).

> Whereunto shall we liken the kingdom of God? or with what comparison shall we compare it?
>
> It is like a grain of mustard seed, which, when it is sown in the earth,

is less than all the seeds that be in the earth:

> But when it is sown, it groweth up, and becometh greater than all herbs, and shooteth out great branches; so that the fowls of the air may lodge under the shadow of it.
>
> Mark 4:30-32

An idea is inspired of God and, like a seed, carries its future within it. Once an idea is released from your heart, it will grow until it becomes a blessing to humanity. Isaiah 55:10 says God's rain (inspiration) gives seed (ideas) to the sower and bread (daily bread) to the eater.

You already have many ideas inside you, but you must acknowledge and release them as God brings them to your attention. A good man, out of the good treasures in his heart, brings forth good things (Matthew 12:35). Inspired ideas will constantly flow through you when you keep your mind renewed by the Word of God and prayer.

7

Add Fuel for Success

Prayer and God's Word are the food of your soul, and your conversation tells others if you have been eating properly.

Finding a secret place of prayer is very important to receiving inspired ideas from God. When you come to God in secret, He rewards you openly. As you dig out God's truths through prayer, He helps you meet your needs.

> But thou, when thou prayest, enter into thy closet, and when thou hast shut thy door, pray to thy Father which is in secret; and thy Father which seeth in secret shall reward thee openly. Matthew 6:6

God wants you to confide your needs to Him. Prayer is a time of communion between you and the Father; it is a time when God opens your eyes and gives you answers.

> Ask, and it shall be given you; seek,
> and ye shall find; knock, and it shall
> be opened unto you.   Matthew 7:7

God will unlock the door of His treasury of blessings to you, if you believe His Word. Many Christians do not know the power in God's Word; therefore, they do not know how to believe.

Prayer and God's Word are the food of your soul, and your conversation tells others if you have been eating properly and shows them the level of your faith.

God's Word inspires faith within you and awakens your inspirations and creativity. When your mind is renewed and your senses are placed on God's altar, you will easily recognize ideas sent from Heaven.

> So then faith cometh by hearing, and
> hearing by the word of God.
> > Romans 10:17

Faith allows you to rely upon God completely, so you can enjoy His blessings. When you come to God by faith, the impossible becomes the possible.

> But without faith it is impossible to
> please him: for he that cometh to God

must believe that he is, and that he is
a rewarder of them that diligently seek
him.   Hebrews 11:6

When you meditate on God's Word, you are
measuring it out and feeding your spirit-man.
This again is like adding fuel to fire.

My heart was hot within me, while I
was musing [meditating] the fire
burned.   Psalm 39:3

Through the Word of God, you draw out of
the divine nature of God which begins to flow
through you.

Whereby are given unto us exceeding
great and precious promises: that by
these ye might be partakers of the
divine nature.   II Peter 1:4

As you meditate on God's Word day and
night, you draw upon truth and become like a
tree planted by a river of inspiration. Your leaf
will not wither when the going gets tough, and
you will bring forth fruit in due season.

Blessed is the man that walketh not in
the counsel of the ungodly, nor
standeth in the way of sinners, nor
sitteth in the seat of the scornful.

But his delight is in the law of the
Lord; and in his law doth he meditate
day and night.

And he shall be like a tree planted
by the rivers of water, that bringeth

> forth his fruit in his season; his leaf
> also shall not wither; and whatsoever
> he doeth shall prosper.
>
> Psalms 1:1-3

I am planted like a tree by the rivers of water, bringing forth fruit in due season. I get my messages, ideas, and revelations as the anointing of God flows through me during prayer and meditation on His Word.

The Word of God sets fire to those Holy Ghost inspirations flowing in your life. His Word contains spiritual vitamins which will cure the ills in your life.

> For they are life to those who find
> them, healing and health to all their
> flesh.   Proverbs 4:22 (AMP)

When you meditate on God's Word, it causes you to ride upon the high places of the earth and eat honey (the strength of life) out of the rock, Christ Jesus (Deuteronomy 32:13; I Corinthians 10:4).

> How sweet are thy words unto my
> taste! yea, sweeter than honey to my
> mouth!   Psalms 119:103

Honey is nature's purest form of energy. Likewise, God's Word is God's purest form of Holy Ghost energy and strength. If you are needing more energy, get fired up in the Word.

In Judges 14:8, Samson found honey in the carcass of a lion, and he ate it for strength and energy. I have found out how to get the honey out of the rock and the carcass of the lion. Both the rock and the lion are symbolic of Jesus. You, too, can dip in and draw honey out of the rock; you can let inspired ideas flow through you.

As you renew your mind by meditating on the promises of God, it releases health and success into every area of your life.

Since thousands of ideas go past you all the time, you need to do something with them.

• **Write your ideas down**

Your memory may fail later. When you write an idea down, you capture it. Then it will crystalize before the devil can steal it from you.

• **Expand on your ideas**

Write down everything you feel might apply to that idea. Later, you may decide to keep those thoughts or to throw them away.

I have ideas that go back as far as five years. Once in a while I go through them and clean them out. It is amazing how many of these ideas I am seeing being accomplished today. I have found that most ideas are just the tip of the iceberg. You would be amazed at what lies underneath the surface.

> First the blade, then the ear, after that
> the full corn in the ear.
>
> Mark 4:28

Is it any wonder the devil is angry and trying to cause God's people problems? Wake up, and refuse to let the devil fool you any longer with his lies. Heaven has come to earth, and you have the keys to loose it into your life.

Perhaps, as you are reading this book, you have suddenly realized that you have never committed your life to Jesus. You are having trouble getting free from the lies of Satan.

In Matthew 16:13-17 Jesus asked His disciples,

> Whom do men say that I the Son of man am?
>
> And they said, Some say that thou art John the Baptist: some, Elias; and others, Jeremias, or one of the prophets.
>
> He saith unto them, But whom say ye that I am?
>
> And Simon Peter answered and said, Thou art the Christ, the Son of the living God.
>
> And Jesus answered and said unto him, Blessed art thou Simon Bar-jona: for flesh and blood [feelings and senses] hath not revealed it unto thee, but my Father which is in heaven.

Let me ask you these same two questions.
- Who do YOU say Jesus is?
- Do you believe that Jesus is the Christ, the Son of God?

If you believe this, then your feelings and your senses (your carnal mind) did not reveal it to you. God revealed it to you. Will you let Jesus be Savior and Lord of your life? Will you let the King of Glory come in, now?

If you have aught or unforgiveness against anyone, just say, ''God, forgive me so that I can be forgiven and the real me—the one You created me to be—can be released.''

Your natural thinking will try to hold you in bondage. The natural man cannot see or understand God. He thinks you evolved from an amoeba. God is greater than that. He created *you*, and put good things inside you. All you have to do is acknowledge Jesus as the Son of God, then ask Him to forgive you of your mistakes and sins. He will forgive you for stepping out of truth and into the dominion of Satan and his lies.

Let's Pray

Lord, we present our senses as a living sacrifice. We put them on the altar of God. We want to be rid of all our preconceived thinking, so we can receive God's abundance. Lord, we will write the Word of God upon our mind, and put it upon the doorpost of our hearts. Then we know our days will be multiplied, and be as the days of Heaven on earth. Now we release the Will of God, as it is in Heaven, into our lives.

Lord, we acknowledge Jesus as Savior. We acknowledge that He is the Son of God.

Yes, we believe He suffered for our sins so we could escape the penalty of sin. We believe Christ is risen from the grave and lives in us.

We know the will of God is being done in us. Now we don't have to beg and plead like a servant, for we are heirs of God. We acknowledge that Christ is the Lord of lords. We confess that Jesus is our Lord. Father, we repent of all murmuring and jealousies. Cleanse us, Jesus, from unrighteousness so Your perfect will can be released through our lives. Amen.

8

Open the Throttle

Anyone can shout and rejoice after
the victory, but it takes faith
to shout before the victory.

There is a place in your life where you can have health, abundant life and financial success. There is a place where you can achieve your goals and realize your dreams. This place is your Jericho, which means *a sweet smelling place*.

You have a Jericho, a sweet place, within you, and we want to release that sweetness out of you. But there are walls, limitations, around your Jericho.

God told Joshua He had given him the *city* of Jericho, not just the walls around the city.

> See, I have given into thine hand Jericho, and the king thereof, and the mighty men of valour   Joshua 6:2

The walls surrounding Jericho limited Joshua's entrance. Are walls surrounding your Jericho? Are there walls keeping you from getting into your sweet smelling place?

- Resentment
- Wrong thinking
- Unforgiveness
- Jealousy
- Strife
- Backbiting
- Carnality

These walls will stop you from acknowledging and harvesting the good things in you. They are carnal walls built by the lies of Satan.

> And I, brethren, could not speak unto you as unto spiritual, but as unto carnal, even as unto babes in Christ.
>
> For ye are yet carnal: for whereas there is among you envying, and strife, and divisions, are ye not carnal, and walk as men?
>
> I Corinthians 3:1-3

The carnal walls of your mind—those strongholds of wrong thinking—must be cast down in order for you to get into your Jericho (II Corinthians 10:4-5).

God had Joshua and the Israelites march around Jericho seven times on the last day and then shout. When they shouted, the walls fell. Like Joshua, you may need to shout down those things that are not in God's will for you.

- Unforgiveness
- Doubt
- Unbelief
- Poverty
- Sickness
- Carnality

When they are totally shouted down, you will be able to get into your Jericho. There are sweet things inside of you which you need to release into the world.

In order to do this, what miracles do you need right now? What is your sweet place in life? What are your dreams? What are your goals? Do you need a happy family, total healing and health, prospering finances, transportation, a good job, a sound mind, a nice car?

Whatever you need, your heavenly Father has the answer waiting for you. The GREAT ''I AM'' is everything you need.

- If you need healing, He's *Jehovah Rapha*, your Healer.
- If you need peace, He's *Jehovah Shalom*, the Prince of Peace.
- If you need finances, He's *Jehovah Jireh*, your Provider.

God has placed His abilities and potential within you and has given you a sweet place to live—a place that is full of His abundance. But the Lord has shown me that the enemy has built walls to discourage you from achieving your maximum potential and receiving your miracles of abundance.

Up until now, these walls have kept you from entering into the sweet-smelling, fragrant place that God has prepared for you. But God has shown me how you and I together can tear down these walls. It's the same plan God gave Joshua in the Old Testament (Joshua 6).

God gave Joshua and the children of Israel the city of Jericho, but they had to go in and possess it. He instructed them to quietly march around the city once every day for six days.

Then on the seventh day, they were to march around Jericho seven times, with the priests blowing the trumpets. On the final round, the children of Israel were to shout and the walls would fall.

When Joshua and the people followed God's instructions exactly and shouted in faith before their victory, the walls that had surrounded their sweet place in life collapsed! Then the Israelites charged in and took the city.

As the children of Israel acted upon the Word of God spoken by His servant, Joshua, they received their sweet place in life.

God gave Joshua the plan and the anointing to break down those walls so that the children of Israel could enter into Jericho, their place of miracles. God has given me the plan and the anointing to help you achieve your maximum potential and enter into your place of God's abundance in your life.

It's the same plan that God wants us to follow today for your needs. Here's how He wants to deliver you and give you the miracles you need today.

First, sit down right now and tell me on the enclosed prayer request page what you want from God. What do you believe your sweet place in life is? Maybe you need an inspired idea, a new beginning, a new car, a marriage, your children's salvation, or to be released from fear. Whatever it is, send me your prayer requests today.

The children of Israel marched around the walls of Jericho seven times. You and I are going to march seven times, in faith, around the sweet place in your life that you tell me about in your prayer requests. We're going to march for *your* victory!

When I receive your list of needs, I'm going to join my faith with yours and believe God for your miracle!

Starting the day you send me your prayer request, at the same time each day, I want you to march quietly around your needs seven times at home. Do this by faith and agree that you will receive your miracle.

On the seventh day, march quietly around your needs six times. Then on the seventh round, boldly shout by faith that you have the victory! Do all of this by faith. I will be agreeing with you for your victory.

The walls of doubt and unbelief, discouragement, unforgiveness, and problems are going to be torn down at the very moment you give your shout of victory.

Together, we're going to believe God for a supernatural, miraculous energizing of your potential. Together, we are going to believe for your miracles. We're going to sound the trumpets and have the music going forward. I believe with all my heart that as we unite together in the praise and worship of God, the powers of darkness are going to be pulled down!

From the moment we shout your victory, miracles are going to begin to happen. Your dreams are going to stir within you and bubble forth. The things that have been missing in your life are going to begin to show up from that moment. There's going to be a healing that will take place in every area of your life.

You may be able to see your miracle instantly, or your situation may amend from that hour. If you do not see any changes with your natural eye right away, know, by faith, that your miracle took place in the spirit realm and that you will see it.

The strongholds of the enemy will be pulled down the very moment you shout for your miracle. Just remember, it may take time for things to change in the natural realm. Don't give up. If you continue in faith and faint not, you will see the fruit of your spoken words come to pass!

Anyone can shout and rejoice *after* the victory, but it takes faith to shout *before* the victory. That's what the children of Israel did; they had the faith to shout before the victory, and the walls of Jericho came tumbling down.

But you must step out in faith, too. One of the most powerful ways of releasing your faith is by worshipping God with your finances. There is something about giving God your money that causes expectancy to spring forth. When you've given God your best, you can expect His best.

That is why I want you to worship God with your best sacrificial offering of $77, $177, $777, or $1777, or more today as your act of faith in advance of your miracle.

Let your gift amount contain the number seven to remind you of this miracle march of faith for releasing the good things God has placed within you.

Your gift will help me reach out to the four corners of the earth with the Gospel of miracle blessings that Jesus wants to give every man, woman, and child on the face of the earth today.

Send your sacrificial gift as an act of faith today. Seed out of your personal finances, out of your business, or however you have to do it; but just do it. Stretch your faith!

You will be releasing what you have in your hands to God and receiving what is in God's hands for you. There is no receiving until there is giving; there is no reaping until there is sowing. When you give you are saying, ''God, I believe that I receive.''

God said that if you vow and pay on your vows (*give* to Him), that you can call upon Him in the day of trouble and He will deliver you (you will *receive* a miracle) (Psalm 50:14-15 NIV).

You see, whatever you believe, you receive. You are receiving now what you have been believing. I am trying to get your faith released, so that you can look beyond what is seen. Joshua saw the victory. I want you to see your victory.

Don't let the devil steal this opportunity. I want you to sit down right now and send your best gift, along with your prayer requests. Tell me what you are believing God for, what is your sweet place in life.

Your perfect miracle, your maximum potential, is there, but the powers of darkness have stood between you and that miracle victory. Together, we're going to tear down those walls the enemy has erected in your life.

Many people miss their victory by looking at their needs; that is all they think about.

However, if they will seek to know God first, they will have their temporal needs met.

Many people wait:
- To have something
- In order to be able to do something
- So they'll be something in life

But they have it backwards. That is not faith; that is walking by sight. God has called us to walk by faith and not by sight (II Corinthians 5:7). He wants you to give even if your natural mind says you can't afford it.

Don't follow men's ways. Follow God's way:
- Be something in Christ (You already are)
- Do something in faith (Give)
- Then you'll have something (Miracles)

Joshua was first the servant of God. Then God told him what to do in order to have what he wanted. It took faith to obey. To the unbeliever, it probably looked foolish. Can you imagine what his enemies were saying? "Do you see Joshua and those Israelites? They think they're going to capture us by marching around our walls!"

Yes, it looked foolish; but the Bible says God uses foolish things to confound the wise, and He uses weak things to confound the mighty (I Corinthians 1:27).

But it all starts with faith in God; you must seek Him first. Look not at the things that are seen, and God said He would give you the things you have need of (Matthew 6:33; II Corinthians 4:18).

Joshua didn't look at the walled city; instead, he listened to God and did what He said to do. God told him what he could have if he looked to God; and when Joshua obeyed, the children of Israel received their miracle!

Stretch your faith today. Look to God, not at your needs. Worship Him with your best gift right now and watch the walls in your life fall down flat. Watch those good things within you come forth.

A Word from the Lord for You

For truly, saith the Lord, as you march every day for seven days around your walls—just as Joshua and the children of Israel marched around the walls of Jericho—your faith will grow and grow each day.

On that final day, that final hour, that final minute, saith the Lord, as you shout, it will be the shout of victory, the shout of faith. And I will cause My angels to go forth to tear down those walls and you will begin to step into your sweet place in life.

For I have ordained this day, saith the Lord, even before the foundations of the world. For this is the hour of great revival and this is just the beginning of the miracles, signs, and wonders that you are going to see in your life in these last days.

What a powerful Word from the Lord that was! God is getting ready to move in a supernatural way like you've never seen before! I sense that in my spirit-man right now.

Please don't miss this mighty move of God. This is only the beginning of your miracle flow in these last days. God is about to show Himself strong on your behalf. Those abilities, talents and dreams which God has placed within you are going to supernaturally energize and change your life. Your friends and neighbors will see what is happening, and they will know that your God is the Almighty God that answers prayer.

The end of your sorrow is near because God has a sweet, fragrant place prepared for you that you have never known before.

Taste the sweetness of the good things He has in store for you right now (Psalm 34:8; Proverbs 24:13). Don't let your miracle get away. Receive it by faith this very moment, grab hold of it. It's yours. Your miracle belongs to you. It has your name on it.

This is an anointed plan that you can't afford to miss. Get started today and GET READY FOR SATAN'S WALLS TO TUMBLE DOWN AND FOR THE REAL YOU TO MARCH IN VICTORIOUS!

9

Full Steam Ahead

Not everyone will pay the price to change their lives. Many continue in unfilled lives, but the following men and women, like you, saw a chance to develop those talents and dreams God had placed within them. For some, the price was great; for all it required faith.

Each of them found that studying God's Word, praying, and following the principles in this book were like shoveling coal into the boiler room of their hearts. The more they meditated on the Word of God, the higher the fires of faith burned within them. The hotter the fires of faith flamed, the more hindrances and walls they pushed aside.

You don't have to stay where you are. You can have everything, be everything and do everything God created you for; you can choose your own destiny as these people did.

D an always dreamed of becoming a police officer. Four different police departments tested him, and he did well on the physical agility and written portions of the exams. But he always ended up getting turned down after the final interview. Dan's dream was beginning to shrivel up and die, when his wife, Barbara, took action.

Barbara tried everything she could think of to help and encourage Dan in the pursuit of his dream. She loved her husband and wanted to see him happy and fulfilled.

One day, while watching my daily television program, Barbara suddenly realized that there was one more thing she could do to help Dan. Immediately, she called our Prayer Line and made a $500 vow of faith to God through this ministry. As the phone minister prayed with her, Barbara had a picture of Jesus calling Lazarus forth from the grave. In her spirit, she could see Dan's dying dream being restored to life.

Barbara felt the yoke of lack being broken off of her family. The depression that had been hanging over their home lifted, and a feeling of happiness and expectancy replaced it. She began paying toward her vow and believing for a miracle.

Dan returned to one of the police departments that had rejected him earlier and took the exam again. After a few months, he received a letter which said that he had done well, but not good enough.

Dan and Barbara didn't lose faith. Instead, they continued to fulfill and pay their vows and to stand on the Word and claim the fulfillment of Dan's dream. Three months later, the department invited him to come back for further testing and interviews. He got accepted into the police academy, and is doing very well! "I know this dream came true because of the covenant we made with the Lord," says Barbara. "If I hadn't made a vow, the dream would have died."

Over a year ago, Marvin made a $100 vow and forgot about it. One day, he was tuned into our program when I mentioned that God takes vowing seriously. Immediately, Marvin repented and began sowing his seed. Money was real tight because he didn't even have a full time job.

Marvin began to seed specifically for a transportation contract with the government. He sent in a bid on a small proposal, but it came in last place. However, he didn't give up. He kept confessing the Word and believing that his dream would come true.

Marvin continued to seed toward his vow, and waited for God to move on his behalf. Soon, he received a letter from the government offering him the chance to bid on a large contract. He prayed and asked the Lord to help him find the right price. He began to work around a figure that came up in his spirit and sent the bid in.

A week later, Marvin received a certified letter saying that before his bid could be accepted, he had to explain how he was going to pay for the truck required in the contract. He was given two weeks to respond. Marvin didn't know what to do. The truck cost $16,000; his credit was bad, and time was running out!

On the last day of the deadline, Marvin still hadn't found a way to purchase the truck, but he felt the Lord telling him to keep believing. The next day, he received a letter rejecting his bid. But, he still held onto his dream, even though the situation looked hopeless.

It wasn't long before Marvin received a letter from me, encouraging him to live in expectancy. That same day, he received a call from the government; they were still interested in his bid!

That Sunday morning Marvin and his family got to church early and were praying in the parking lot, when he noticed a truck parked down the street. It was exactly what he needed! When he found the owner, the man not only agreed to sell the truck, but he offered to finance it too! Now, Marvin's dream is a reality; the $50,000 contract is his!

Don and Susan were away from God and miserable. On the surface, they appeared to have everything going for them. They lived in a nice home and drove a fancy new car, but inside they were spiritually bankrupt. They didn't realize that God wanted to bless every area of their lives.

When Don and Susan first discovered *Success-N-Life*, they were working in one of the bridal shops owned by Susan's parents. They rededicated their lives to God and became monthly *Success-N-Life* partners. Inspired by the tapes and reading materials received from this ministry, they became excited about getting into the Word.

Don and Susan started sensing that God wanted them to move to a different city. When Susan's parents offered to sell them a bridal shop in that city, they felt peace about it and accepted the offer.

Two weeks later, Don and Susan moved; their income doubled, and they bought a house twice the size of the one they left. But they became so content with their new home and business, that they forgot about God. A month later, they found themselves in a dry place and realized that they had to seek God first in order to lead abundant, fulfilled lives. They made a decision to seek God three hours a day, no matter what. For the next four months, they spent three hours each night reading the Bible, listening to tapes and praying before going to bed. They did this even if they didn't get home until midnight!

During this time of seeking God with all of his heart, God showed Don a way to create and manufacture bridal veils. Don's previous attempts at making bridal veils were failures, but NOW his new designs can be found in bridal shops throughout the United States!

Don and Susan also awakened their faith through vowing. When they put their house up for sale, it was on the market for six months, and it looked like it might be there a lot longer. God revealed to Susan that she needed to make and pay a $500 vow for the sale of their house. Susan called our prayer line and made the vow, and paid it immediately. Fifteen days later, a couple looked at the house and offered to buy it. Three days later, they closed the deal!

Then, a time came when Don and Susan had $30,000 worth of inventory debt. They needed to be out of debt before they went to market, and that was only a few weeks away. Don felt led to make and pay a $1,000 vow for a successful sale. In just fourteen days, they made $32,000! "When you obey God, you can't go wrong!" exclaims Don.

Soon after Connie got saved, she discovered our daily television program. Severe backaches had plagued her for 15 years; she couldn't even stand up straight! When

Connie heard me talk about my healing tapes, she felt like they were exactly what she needed.

As soon as the tapes arrived, Connie began listening to them eight hours a day. She knew that her healing lay in the Word of God. One day, as she sat on her couch, the Lord told her she was healed. Her backaches disappeared and have never returned!

Connie received one miracle; several months later she needed another one! Her husband, Chester, had been laid off for a month. He was a construction worker, and business was slow. Convinced that my message was from God, she stepped out in faith and made a $500 vow, believing that Chester would find work.

The day after Connie made her vow, Chester started working on a job that would take six weeks to complete! And she began seeding toward her vow. When the job was finished, Connie released her faith for more work by increasing her vow to $1,000.

Things started to slow down, and Chester couldn't find work. He tried other types of jobs, but none of them were right for him. Connie was getting discouraged when she heard an inspiring testimony on our program. Faith leaped in her heart. She cried out to God, reminding Him that she had made and seeded toward a vow.

The very next day, Chester found another construction job! He also received a phone call from a friend, who told him about a supervisory position that had just opened. Chester called the company and mailed them his application. Chester got the job, and soon, he was in a position to hire the friend that gave him the lead!

Yolanda had a spiritual void in her life. She felt like she was missing God's plan because things weren't happening for her and her husband, Juan. Financial problems filled their home with tension, and she and Juan were constantly arguing with each other.

No matter how hard Yolanda tried, she couldn't come up with answers to solve their financial problems. Juan had a maintenance job, but it didn't pay enough to meet their needs. Unpaid bills started piling up, and it looked like they were going to lose their car and apartment. For over a year, Juan had been trying to find work with the Postal Service. He had taken the examination twice, but no one ever called him about the results. It looked hopeless.

When Yolanda first started watching my daily television program, she was skeptical. But each time she tried to turn the channel, she found herself sitting back down to watch some more. One day I said, ''There's a young lady who is watching, and she and her husband have been believing for a certain job. You need to get up and make a vow right now!'' Yolanda knew that this Word was from God. Immediately, she went to the phone, called our Prayer Ministry Center, and made a $200 vow.

Just one week after Yolanda released her faith through vowing, Juan got an unexpected call from the Post Office. They told him that if he still wanted the job it was his! All he had to do was come in and fill out the paperwork!

As Yolanda and Juan paid toward their vow, other miracles began to take place in their lives. In less than two months, they were caught up on all their bills! The strife and tension that filled their home has been replaced by a gentle peace. Yolanda says, ''I realized where I was lacking spiritually in my life when I started receiving the teaching about giving out of my need and expecting a return.''

When Mike's wife left and took their two children, his world began to fall apart. Severe depression and loneliness set in. He started having horrible ''death dreams,'' in which he saw himself burning or exploding into tiny pieces. Mike thought he was going insane.

Attitude problems and a drop in his work performance led to Mike's resignation from the military. He was able to find a job as a computer technician, but he never seemed to have enough money to pay his bills. He was convinced that he would never have a nice home and car, and that he would always be in debt. Life didn't seem worth living.

Finally, Mike was driven to the edge. He couldn't stand living in constant mental anguish. He was contemplating suicide, when a Christian friend invited him over and started witnessing to him. As Mike listened, a healing began to take place, and his depression began to lift.

When Mike discovered our daily television program, he felt the Spirit move within him to complete that healing. He watched our program every day, and as he received exposure to the Word of God, a dramatic change began to take place in his life. His attitude improved, and the loneliness vanished; even his co-workers noticed the change!

Excited about the transformation that was taking place in his life, Mike made and began seeding toward a $1,000 vow for God's blessings. In just a few weeks, his lifestyle improved dramatically. He was able to acquire a car and a lakefront home, pay all his bills, and a growth on his shoulder disappeared! Now, he looks forward to life! "My faith in God continues to grow through your ministry," writes Mike.

This book has shown you how to release the good things and great desires God has placed within you. It has shown you how to get rid of the walls that are stopping you from reaching your maximum potential and being what God created you to be.

Most of all, this book has shown you how to shovel the coal of God's Word into the boiler room of your heart, to fuel your faith so that you can achieve any dream.

Now it is up to you to shout the victory and to taste the sweetness of the good things God has in store for you. All it takes is faith. One of the most powerful ways of releasing your faith is by vowing and giving to God. When you plant your money, somehow it causes expectancy to spring forth. Also, when you put God first and give Him your best, you take the limits off Him and allow Him to give you His best.

You believe that tucked away in your heart is more than you presently see in your life. You feel that you are worth more and can achieve more than you are achieving now. I believe that is why you read this book: God ordained that you learn the principles of releasing those good things He has placed within you.

You will be choosing your own destiny today when you put the principles in this book into operation, give God your best gift, and let Him help you become all you can be. Do it now! Then, write me and tell me about your successes. I want you to have everything, be everything and do everything God created you for.

My dear friend, before you lay this book aside, make sure you put God first so you too may have the desires of your heart.

First, ask Jesus to cleanse you of your sins. You don't have to clean up your life first—God will do it for you. He will also give you a new heart, new desires, and the Spirit of truth.

If you follow these new desires—which are based on God's Word—you will have a beautiful new life on Earth, and eternal life.

Pray this prayer out loud and believe:

"Father in Heaven, I've heard Your Word, and I want to be born again. Jesus, cleanse me of my sins. I want to be a child of God. I want to give my life to You. Make me a new person. Be my Lord and Savior.

"I believe I'm now born again, because the Word of God says I am! Jesus is my Lord. Thank You, Jesus, for a new life. Amen."

Now, don't go by what you think or feel. Go by what God's Word says. You are saved—you are born again. Believe it!

If you prayed this prayer sincerely, then call us at our 24-hour prayer line—(214) 620-6200—and a prayer-minister will help you. Or, write for more information (with no obligation):

"Salvation Information"
Robert Tilton Ministries • P. O. Box 819000 • Dallas, Texas 75381
In Canada: P.O. Box 4900 • Vancouver, BC V6B 4A6

ORDER FORM

QTY

☐ **Biblical Success Course**
Successful—spirit, soul and body. Robert Tilton shows you how in these tapes.
$100 (12 tapes)

$ _____
T152

☐ **Total Healing & Health**
Let Robert Tilton show you how to release your faith so that you, too, can walk in divine health.
$100 (12 tapes)

$ _____
T153

☐ **To Catch A Thief**
Seven for one is what Satan must return for the things he steals from you. Learn how to force him to pay up!
$20 (4 tapes)
Plus Free Book

$ _____
510

TOTAL

$ _____
FYB

Canadian Partners—Please add 20%

RETURN THIS WITH YOUR FULL PAYMENT

To make your vow call [214] 620-6200 or write:
Robert Tilton Ministries • P.O. Box 819000 • Dallas, TX 75381
In Canada: P.O. Box 4900 • Vancouver, BC V6B 4A6

Name _____

Address _____

City _____ State _____

Zip _____ Phone (_____) _____

All funds are used for designated projects and for the worldwide ministry in accordance with Ezra 7:17-18.

ROBERT TILTON MINISTRIES
Miracle Prayer Requests

☐ Please pray and agree with me about the pressing needs in my life.

☐ I have given unto the work of God. I believe He will open the windows of Heaven unto me, and rebuke the devourer from my life, according to Malachi 3:10-11.

☐ My specific needs are:

_____

_____

_____

_____

_____

_____

_____

RETURN THIS FOR PRAYER

Name _____

Address _____

City _____ State _____

Zip _____ Phone (_____) _____

Robert Tilton Ministries • P.O. Box 819000 • Dallas, TX 75381
In Canada: P.O. Box 4900 • Vancouver, BC V6B 4A6

If you have a testimony of how our monthly books and tapes have changed your life, please write and tell me about it. Send a snapshot of yourself, too.

_____

_____

_____

_____

_____

_____

_____

_____

_____

_____

_____

_____

_____

_____

Name _____

Address _____

City _____ State _____ Zip _____

Phone _____

Use order form on page 106.

Use order form on page 106.

Use order form on page 106.